Creative Crafts
Using
Your Computer

Other Titles of Interest

Creative Crafts Using Your Computer

By
J. Cleverly

Bernard Babani (publishing) Ltd
The Grampians
Shepherds Bush Road
London W6 7NF
England

www.babanibooks.com

Please Note

Although every care has been taken with the production of this book to ensure that any projects, designs modifications, information and/or programs, etc., contained herewith operate in a correct and safe manner and also that any components or materials specified are normally available in Great Britain, the Publishers and Author(s) do not accept responsibility in any way for the failure (including fault in design) of any project design, modification or program to work correctly or to cause damage to any equipment that it may be connected to or used in conjunction with, or in respect of any other damage or injury that may be caused, nor do the Publishers or Author(s) accept responsibility in any way for the failure to obtain specified components or materials.

Notice is also given that if equipment that is still under warranty is modified in any way or used or connected with home-built equipment then that warranty may be void.

© 2006 BERNARD BABANI (publishing) LTD
First Published – August 2006

British Library Cataloguing in Publication Data:
A catalogue record for this book is available from the British Library

ISBN 0 85934 568 8

Cover Design by Gregor Arthur
Printed and Bound in Great Britain by Cox & Wyman Ltd., Reading

About this Book

Creative Crafts using your computer was written specifically for the purpose of exploring the more creative side of the computer. Everything you need to know to get you started creating professional looking crafts is contained in this book.

Most people who own a computer already have the necessary equipment to get started crafting at home. A small outlay might be needed to purchase printer media and art materials required for certain projects but again it depends on the project undertaken.

The intent of this book is to empower, inspire and aid you in your hobby, craft or small business enterprise. Both beginners and experienced computer users can enjoy adding to their knowledge in a fun and productive way.

The instructions inside guide you through the printer media and paper available for crafts and hobbies. The art and craft equipment required. The manipulation of text and images on the computer, and a variety of projects to try, which contain the instructions on how to use the printer media to make the crafts. Choose a project, dip into the relevant sections of the book and enjoy computer crafting.

Trademarks

Microsoft, Windows XP and Office 2003, are either registered trademarks or trademarks of Microsoft Corporation.

All other brand and product names used in the book are recognised as trademarks, or registered trademarks, of their respective companies. There is no intent to use the trademarks generically and readers should investigate ownership of a trademark before using it for any purpose.

About the Author

Julie Cleverly spent 16 years working in the I.T industry during which time she undertook training courses at IBM, ICL, and Digital Computers. After taking a short break to start a family she undertook a teacher training course and completed a Certificate of Education at Portsmouth University. She currently develops, writes, and presents Information Computing Technology courses for a wide variety of clients, including schools, colleges, adult education, individuals, small groups and businesses.

Warning

Children should only use scissors, knives, irons or any other possibly hazardous implements under the supervision of a responsible adult.

Contents

Introduction

Introduction

Creative Crafts Using Your Computer is designed for everyone who is interested in creating and enhancing crafts by using a computer. No experience is necessary in either computing or crafting, as clear step by step instructions are used throughout this book.

All you need to enjoy creative computer crafting is a computer with Microsoft Word 2003 installed and either an inkjet or laser printer. An Internet connection is useful for obtaining images and text.

A few of the projects use a Scanner and Digital Camera primarily to obtain images. A scanner and digital camera are not essential as other sources of images can be used such as Microsoft Clip Art, which is part of Microsoft Word 2003 or picture, text and image CD ROMs.

Creative Crafts Using Your Computer uses images and pictures readily available to all on Microsoft clip art to demonstrate the techniques of manipulating images and text, and clearly explains how to use your computer as an aid to creating and designing crafts.

Learn how to print your designs onto a range of computer papers and media, including fabric sheets, shrink paper and magnetic paper. Create stencils and templates used in many craft activities. Learn how to transfer images, designs and text onto a variety of products including ceramics, and candles.

Try some quick and easy projects, which are fun for children as well as adults, such as Fridge Magnets, Shrink Jewellery or Window Stickers. Or, try more intricate and time consuming projects like Gift Boxes, Appliqué and Embroidery pictures.

Create individual personal gifts, or decorate a room by using themes to make matching items such as tablecloths, egg cups, napkin rings, curtains, flowerpots, placemats, coasters and mugs, or create a matching set of T-shirts for yourself and your friends.

Experiment by mixing and matching the materials and techniques shown in Crafts Using Your Computer and create something entirely new.

Most of all be inspired, enjoy experimenting, creating and playing.

Art and Craft Materials

Art and Craft Materials

Art and Craft Materials used for the projects are:

Scissors, Craft Knife and Mat

A craft knife and mat are useful but not essential for the projects in this book. A large pair of scissors for general use and a pair of smaller scissors for more detailed and precise work are just as suitable.

Ruler and Tape Measure

Use for measuring the boxes, card apertures and T-shirts.

Acrylic Varnish and Acrylic Spray Varnish

The quick drying acrylic varnish is used for protecting the decoupage, paint and the finished craft work. The spray acrylic varnish is essential when using water slip decals to stop the ink from floating off when immersed in water.

PVA and Paper Glue

All the glue has to be water based. PVA glue is white and thicker than paper glue and dries clear.Use the PVA glue to stick the shrink butterflies and heavier items in place. The paper glue is clear, runny and similar to wallpaper paste. Use the paper glue to stick the decoupage images down.

Acrylic Paint

Acrylic paint is very versatile and dries quickly. It can be used straight from the tube or diluted with water. To keep the paint from drying out in between coats cover with a damp cloth.

Paintbrushes

Different sizes of small paintbrushes and one 3" paintbrush for applying base coats to larger items.

Soft Cloth and Roller

A small roller for applying decoupage and decals to prevent air bubbles is very useful, as is a soft cloth for smoothing air bubbles and excess water from decals.

Useful Items

Other useful items include: a **Bowl of Water** for water slip decals. **Fusible Bonding Web** used for the fabric bag, and appliqué scene. An **Iron** for T-shirt transfers. **Tin Foil**, a **Baking Tray** and a **Heavy Book** for the shrink paper process. Different sized **Needles,** and most essential when using paint, glue and water **Kitchen Roll**.

Items to Decorate

Items to decorate can include wooden plaques, glasses, ceramics, candles, bags, cardboard boxes, clay flowerpots, Aida, greetings cards, hairclips, badges, teapots, T-shirts, and fabrics.

Embellishments

Embellish your work by adding beads, tapestry wools, embroidery silks, leather thongs, jewellery wire, sequins, and glitter.

Computer Resources

Computer Resources

Microsoft Word 2003

Microsoft Word 2003 can be purchased separately or as part of the Microsoft Office Suite. It is readily available from most computer shops and computer retailers.

Internet

The Internet is a very good resource for acquiring graphic images and text. There are plenty of web sites offering downloads for images, photographs, cartoons, and fonts. Some of the web sites are free and others you need to subscribe to. It is important to be aware of the copyright regulations both at home and abroad when using the Internet to source images.

Lists of suppliers for craft products, computer paper and inks can be found on the Internet. Most of the online retailers offer online shopping facilities as well as online craft chat rooms and forums, who supply useful help and advice on craft projects and techniques.

Scanner

A scanner can be used to copy images, text, photographs, fabric, shapes, paintings and anything that will fit on it. The scanned in image can then be transferred to various computer programs such as Microsoft Word or a graphics program. The image can then be manipulated or printed directly onto different printer papers and computer media.

Digital Camera

Take your own photographs and use them to decorate mouse mats, fridge magnets, mugs, and tea towels. Or turn your photographs into calendars and greetings cards.

CD's

CD's containing, images, graphics, art, clip art, photographs, and text fonts can be purchased from computer retailers and high street shops. Subject specific CD's such as patterns and backgrounds can be purchased online.

Copyright

Work created by another person is copyrighted. The author or creator of the work has the right to control the way the work is used or changed. Downloading from the Internet and copying images from magazines and books could mean you are infringing the author's copyright. Some authors will charge a fee for the use of their work, while other authors and websites offer copyright free material. More advice about copyright is available on the Internet and in the public library.

Printers

Both inkjet and laser printers can be used to create crafts on your computer. Paper products and media are available for both laser and inkjet printers. When buying paper products and media ensure it is suitable for the type of printer you have.

Inks

For craft projects use waterproof, fade resistant and smudge resistant computer ink cartridges.

Paper Sizes

Computer paper and media is available in different sizes. The most common are:

A3 = 297 x 420 mm
A4 = 210 x 297 mm
A5 = 148 x 210 mm

Before buying paper and media refer to your printer guide for instructions on using the different paper sizes in your printer.

Paper and Printer Media Products

Printer paper and media is a general heading covering a wide range of products, some of which are obviously not paper-like in look or feel at all. The computer papers use a special coating that allows the ink or toner to stick to the paper, if you use untreated paper the results may not be the same as using the treated paper. Here is a list of some of the products available to put through your printer and some suggestions for their use.

Plain Computer Paper

Plain computer paper is used for test printing and some decoupage projects.

Fabric Sheets

Fabric sheets are available for inkjet and laser printers. They come in different sizes, colours, and materials.

Voile, Linen, Silk, Cotton and Canvas fabric sheets are available. The Cotton sheets come in plain cotton, iron-on cotton, or adhesive backed cotton. Most fabric sheets are washable except for the adhesive backed cotton.

Fabric sheet products can be used to make quilts, cards, cushions, dolls, clothing, bags, appliqué, embroidery, patchwork, curtains, tablecloths and many more textile related crafts.

Shrink Paper

Print your design onto shrink paper put it in the oven and it will shrink down and become hard. Use shrink paper for jewellery such as earrings and brooches or for making badges, cards, beads and buttons.

Shrink paper comes in white or clear. When buying shrink paper remember printers do not print in white ink. The colour white will not show on clear paper.

Watercolour Paper

Print onto the watercolour paper and you have an instant watercolour painting. A wide range of fine art papers with a special coating for use with inkjet printers are available through internet suppliers. Use for cards, pictures photographs, and calendars.

Heat Transfer Paper

Heat transfer paper is available for inkjet and laser printers, and for light and dark fabrics. Heat transfer paper is mainly used for transferring images onto fabrics but can also be used for transferring images onto jigsaws, mouse mats, and coasters. Use for quilts, cushions, aprons, curtains and T-shirts. Some makes of heat transfer paper require you to reverse the image before printing.

Window Cling

Window Cling is great for quick projects with children. Print them off uncoloured and let the children decorate them. Use for car window stickers, advertising, decorating, and stained glass window effects.

Magnetic Paper

Magnetic paper is thicker than ordinary computer paper. Put one sheet in at a time when printing. Use for glossy fridge magnets and magnetic games.

Glossy Photo Paper

Glossy photo paper is very versatile but smudges very easily, leave the print to dry thoroughly before touching the paper. Use for printing photographs, calendars, greetings cards and for very shiny projects.

Adhesive Paper

Adhesive backed computer paper. Peel off the backing and stick on to a surface. Use for book plates, stickers, greetings cards, labels and to make templates to stick directly on to a surface to cut around.

Mouse Mats, Coasters and Jigsaw Puzzles

Mouse mats, coasters and jigsaw puzzles are available in different shapes and sizes. Use for photographs or special occasions like birthday parties, Christmas or weddings. Choose a theme such as animals, or flowers and create table mats to match the coasters.

Tattoo Paper

Design and make your own temporary tattoos, use for adults and children's parties, holidays, fancy dress and for fun.

Decoupage Paper

Decoupage papers with a good finish are available for inkjet printers. Use this paper for card making or try using glossy photo paper. If you are going to varnish the decoupage then use ordinary plain computer paper.

Decal Paper

Decal paper is available for inkjet and laser printers. There are two types of decal paper, water slide decals or dry rub-off decals. Both come in clear or white.

Use the water slide decal paper to put images and graphics onto glass, ceramics, metal, candles, plastic, and enamel.

The dry rub-off decals can be used to put images and lettering on the same media as the water slide decal paper but can also be used on wood, cards, paper bags and soap.

Fuzzy Paper and Sticky Fluffy Paper

Use for fuzzy photographs, dolls' house furnishings, upholstery, toys, trains, cars and greetings cards.

Acetate

Use for stencils and cards.

Vellum

Translucent vellum is available in a variety of colours with special effects such as iridescent, metallic, and marble. Use for stained glass and card making.

Microsoft Office Word 2003

Open a Word Document

Microsoft Office Word 2003 is the computer program used in this book to design and print the images and text for the craft projects. There are different ways of opening a Microsoft Office Word 2003 Document.

Fig.1 Desktop Window

On the **Desktop**, the screen that appears when you first switch on your computer, **right-click** on the **Microsoft Office Word 2003** shortcut icon.

Left-click on **Open.**

Fig.2 Open Menu

If the **Microsoft Word 2003** shortcut icon is not on your Desktop, left-click on **Start** at the bottom left-hand corner of the screen. Left-click on **Microsoft Office Word 2003.** **Or** left-click on **Start**, **All Programs, Microsoft Word.** If you have the Office suite installed left-click on **Start, All Programs, Microsoft Office, Microsoft Word**.

Fig.3 Start Menu

Close a Microsoft Office Word 2003 Document

Left-click on the **white cross** in a **red background** in the top right corner of the Microsoft Office Word 2003 window.

If you have not saved the document the computer will ask you if you want to save the document.

Left-click on **Yes** if you want to save the document.

Left-click on **No** if you do not want to save the document.

If you have opened a document and made some changes left-click on **Yes** and the changes to the document will be saved.

If you have opened a document and made some changes you do not want to save left-click on **No** and the changes to the document will not be saved. The original document before the changes will still be saved.

Left-click on **Cancel** to carry on working on the document.

Saving Your Work

Save your work for future use and reference or to retrieve and amend at a later date.

There are two ways of saving your work.
Left-click on the **Save icon** on the standard
toolbar.
Or left-click on **File, Save.**

If it is the first time you have saved the piece of work or document the **Save As** window will appear.

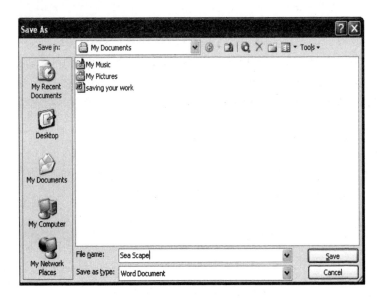

Fig.4 Save As window

The **Save In** box should say **My Documents,** if not left-click on the ∨ next to the **Save In box**: A drop-down menu will provide a list of places and devices on the computer you can save your work to.

Left-click on **My Documents** to select it. **My Documents** will then appear in the **Save In:** box.

In the **File Name:** box type in the name of the piece of work or document, this is the name it will be saved as and used to find later.

Left-click on **Save.** The **Save As** window will disappear and your work or document will be saved.

Save Changes

If you make any changes to your work and want to re-save the work with the changes left-click on the Save icon or left-click on **File, Save.** The changes will be saved but the **Save As** window will not appear.

Retrieving the Work Document

There are two ways of finding your saved work/document.

On the **Desktop**, the screen that appears when you first switch your computer on, right-click on the **My Documents** icon.

Fig.5 Desktop Window

Left-click on **Open.**

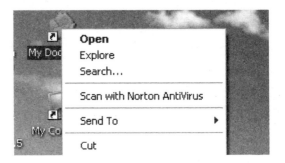

Fig.6 Open Menu

Or:

On the Desktop.
Left-click on **Start.**
Left-click on **My Documents.**

Fig.7 Start Menu

Either way the My Documents window will pop up.

Fig.8 My Documents Window

Open the document ready for use by putting your mouse pointer over the document you want to open and right-click. On the drop-down menu left-click on **Open**. The document will pop up on the screen.

If you want different versions of the same document left-click on **File** and **Save As**. In the **Filename** box, delete the original name and put in the new name, you will have two copies, one with the original name and a second copy with a different name. This is very useful when you are using the same template or design and are changing colours and sizes.

Copying your work or a document will keep the original and save you having to redo all your work. You can then add changes, colours, sizes, and text to the copied document. Save the new copied document as, for instance, Pink Boxes 2 or Blue boxes 1.

Copy a Document

Save the document by first giving it a filename e.g. Pink Boxes.

On the Keyboard hold down the **CTRL key** and then press the **A key**. The whole document should be highlighted, turned black.

Fig.9 Menu Bar

With the highlighting on, left-click on **Edit** on the **Menu** bar.

Left-click on **Copy** on the drop-down menu, or press **Ctrl and C** on the keyboard.

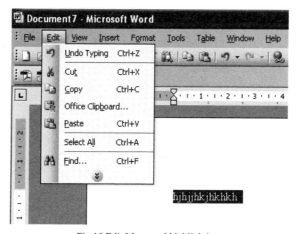

Fig.10 Edit Menu and highlighting

Left-click on the **New Blank Document** icon, under the word **File**.

When the new document has opened on the screen:

Left-click on **Edit** on the **Menu Bar** in the **New Document**

Left-click on **Paste** on the drop-down menu, or press **Ctrl and V** on the keyboard.

Take the Highlighting off by placing the mouse pointer anywhere on the white of the document and left-clicking once.

You can then make changes and re-save the document as, for instance, Pink Boxes with yellow hearts.

Undoing Mistakes

We all make mistakes, luckily Microsoft Word
realises this. On the Standard Toolbar is an icon
called **UNDO**.

The Undo icon stores a list of your most recent actions.

As soon as you have made an error of any kind
left-click on the **Undo** icon.

When you have used the Undo icon the
Redo icon appears next to it.

If you have left-clicked on the Undo icon and gone too far
in undoing your actions, left-click on the **Redo** icon to go
forward again

.

Manipulating Images

The Toolbars

Setting up the toolbars before you start work can save you time and frustration. A quick click on the option displayed on the toolbar means there will be little need to search through menus looking for the option you require. Display the toolbars around the edges of your document available for immediate use. The five main toolbars used to manipulate images and texts are: **Standard, Formatting, Drawing, Picture,** and **Tables and Borders**.

To check and display the toolbars available in the Word Window:

Left-click on **View**; a drop-down menu will appear. Choose **Toolbars.** A list of toolbars will be displayed. Check that a tick appears next to **Standard, Formatting, Drawing, Picture,** and **Tables and Borders**.

If a tick is not displayed left-click on the toolbar name required. The toolbar menu will disappear and the toolbar itself will appear on the screen. To remove the toolbar from display, repeat the above and left-click on the toolbar name to remove the tick.

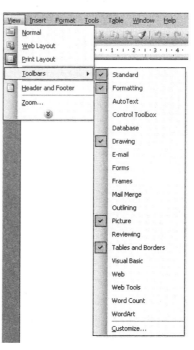

Fig.11 Toolbar Menu

Moving Toolbars

If the toolbar appears in the middle of the document, move it to the edge of the document by placing the mouse pointer over the blue title line. The blue title line has the name of the toolbar on it. Left-click and hold your mouse button down. A four-pointed arrow head will appear. Still holding your mouse button down drag the toolbar to the bottom right (or where there is a space) of your screen and let go of the mouse button. The toolbar will move to the new position.

Fig.12 Toolbar displayed on a document

Fig.13 Moved Toolbar

The Standard Toolbar

The standard toolbar is used to save, print, cut, copy and paste your work. It has a very useful function called print preview which allows you to display your work and zoom in and out before you print it.

The Formatting Toolbar

The formatting toolbar is used to change text, size, and position, embolden, italicise, underline, colour, and add borders.

The Drawing Toolbar

The drawing toolbar is used to access WordArt and Auto shapes, insert pictures and clip art, draw lines, arrows, add shadows and 3D effects.

The Picture Toolbar

The picture toolbar is used to crop, rotate and alter the contrast and brightness of pictures. It also enables you to wrap text around pictures.

The Tables and Borders Toolbar

The tables and borders toolbar is used to create tables and borders, draw lines, delete lines, and change the colour and thickness of lines and borders

Hover Help

As you use the toolbars and functions you will begin to remember where the options are, until then a very useful aid is the Hover Help function. To use Hover Help place your mouse pointer under any of the toolbar icons and wait. Do not click the mouse button. The function of the icon will be displayed.

Margins

Changing the margins allows you more control over the position and amount of text and images on the document. The Margins on Microsoft Word 2003 are preset. The top and bottom margins are set to 2.54 cm, and the left and right margins are set to 3.17 cm. To change the margins left-click on **File**, then left-click on **Page Setup**.

In the **Page Setup** window you can increase the margins by clicking on ▲ and decrease the margins by clicking on ▼. The Preview pane in the bottom right of the Page Setup Window, will change accordingly as you change the margins and paper orientation to give you a preview of the new layout.

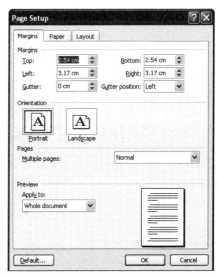

Fig.14 Page Setup Window

Paper Orientation

Set the paper orientation by left-clicking in the **Landscape** or **Portrait** box, in the Page Setup window.

Left-click on **OK** to apply the changes.

Inserting Clip Art

There are two ways of inserting clip art.
Left-click on the **clip art icon** on the drawing toolbar.
Or left-click on **Insert**, **Picture**, and **Clip Art.**

A window appears on the right side of the screen.

In the **Search for box**: type in the name of the picture or image being searched for.

In the **Search In box**: Left-click on the ∨ next to the search in box. Left-click in the box next to the option required. A tick appears to show you have selected that option.

Fig.16 Clip Art Search Criteria

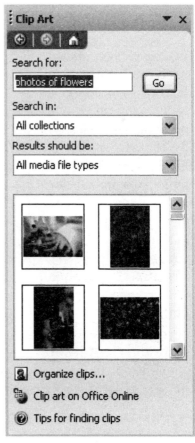

Fig.15 Clip Art Window

In the **Results should be box:** Left-click on the ▼ next to the Results should be box. Left-click in the box next to the required media e.g. Clip Art to put a tick in the box.

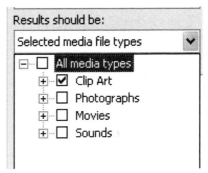

Fig.17 Clip Art Results Menu

If you just want photographs put a tick in the Photographs box and take the tick off the Clip Art box by left-clicking on it.

After you have selected your criteria, left-click on **Go**.

Use the scroll bar to view the selected clip art. Left-click on the ▲ ▼ up and down arrows.

When you have chosen your clip art **insert** it by left-clicking on it.

The chosen clip art will be placed in the Word document.

Fig.18 Displayed Clip Art

Clip Art Online

Microsoft have selections of clip art and photographs you can download from the Internet. In the Clip Art window left-click on **Clip art on Office Online.**

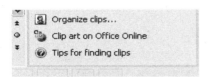

The **Clip Art and Media** page is displayed.

Left-click on ▼ next to the **Search box**. Left-click on a category from the drop-down menu.

In the next box type in the name of the image you are searching for e.g. shells. Left-click on **Go** to initiate the search. Alternatively scroll down the Clip Art and Media web page and select a category from the list displayed.

Fig.19 Clip Art Online Categories List

When you have chosen a category or clicked on Go the clip art is displayed. The number of pages of clip art available to view and download is shown on the bottom right. To view the next page left-click on the ⇨ arrow, and to go back a page left-click on the ⇦ arrow.

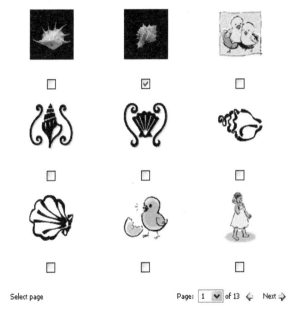

Fig.20 How Clip Art is displayed online

Left-click in the box below the clip art you require. A tick appears to indicate your selection. You can select many items on various pages to download.

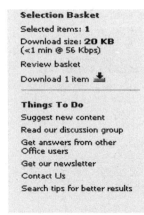

Selection Basket
Selected items: **1**
Download size: **20 KB**
(<1 min @ 56 Kbps)
Review basket
Download 1 item

Things To Do
Suggest new content
Read our discussion group
Get answers from other Office users
Get our newsletter
Contact Us
Search tips for better results

Fig.21 Selection Basket

The clip art you have selected will be added to the **Selection Basket**.

When you have finished choosing the clip art, left-click on the ↓ next to **Download Item**.

If it is the first time you have used clip art on line you will be asked to accept the terms and conditions of use. If you do accept the terms and conditions the download screen appears.
The Download software will choose a Clip Art version for you depending on the software installed on your computer. Left-click on **Download Now**.

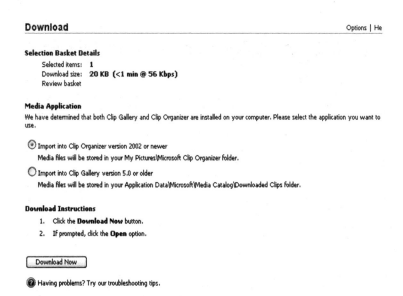

Download   Options | He

Selection Basket Details
    Selected items: **1**
    Download size: **20 KB** (<1 min @ 56 Kbps)
    Review basket

Media Application
We have determined that both Clip Gallery and Clip Organizer are installed on your computer. Please select the application you want to use.

○ Import into Clip Organizer version 2002 or newer
    Media files will be stored in your My Pictures\Microsoft Clip Organizer folder.

○ Import into Clip Gallery version 5.0 or older
    Media files will be stored in your Application Data\Microsoft\Media Catalog\Downloaded Clips folder.

Download Instructions
    1. Click the **Download Now** button.
    2. If prompted, click the **Open** option.

[Download Now]

Ⓗ Having problems? Try our troubleshooting tips.

Fig.22 Clip Art Online Download Menu

A **File Download** window will pop up asking if you want to open the clip art file. Left-click on **Open**.

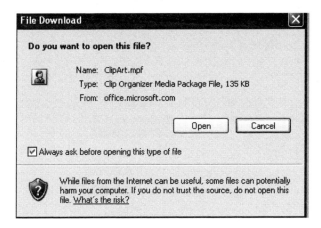

Fig.23 File Download Window

The clip art will be placed in the **Downloaded clips folder** on your computer.

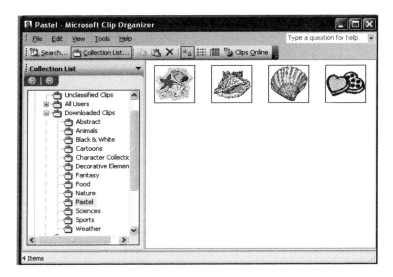

Fig.24Clip Organiser Window

Left-click on the **X** in the top right-hand corner of the **Microsoft Organiser Window** to close it. Left-click on the **X** in the top right-hand corner of the **Office Online Window** to close it.

To include the clip art when you next do a search click on the **▼** next to the **Search in:** box and put a tick in the **Everywhere** box. This will search the clip art folders on your computer for all your saved clips wherever they are. Insert as normal.

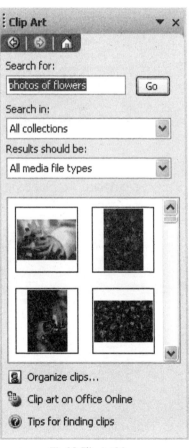

Fig.25 Clip Art Menu

Fig.26 Clip Art Search in options

Inserting Your Own Images and Pictures

There are two ways of inserting your own images and pictures.
Left-click on the **insert picture icon** on the drawing toolbar. Or left-click on **Insert, Picture**, and **From File**.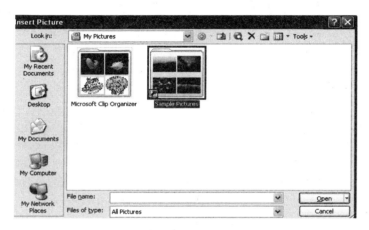

Fig.27 Insert Picture Window (My Pictures)

Left-click on the file or folder required, then left-click on **Open**.

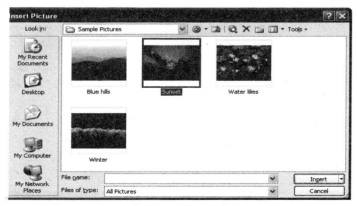

Fig.28 Insert Picture Window (Sample Pictures)

Left-click on the picture required, and then left-click on **Insert**.

Moving Clip Art and Pictures

Before inserting the clip art or picture, place your cursor in the approximate position you want the clip art or picture to be. After insertion use the **Space Bar** and **Return Key** to move the clip art.

Resizing Clip Art and Pictures

Click on the picture or clip art, small square boxes (grabs) appear around the outside. Put your cursor on a box and a two-headed arrow will appear. When the arrow appears left-click and hold your mouse button down. Make the picture larger or smaller by dragging the arrow in or out.

Fig.29 Grabs switched on and two-headed arrow displayed

Deleting Clip Art and Pictures

Left-click on the picture to put the grabs on. Press the delete key.

Copying and Pasting Clip Art

The skull and crossbones clip art below is to be used for decoupage gift boxes at a children's pirate themed party. The clip art was inserted into an exact fit text box based on measurements taken from a box lid. After a test print confirmed the clip art was the correct size for the lids, the text box containing the clip art was copied and pasted for the number of lids required.

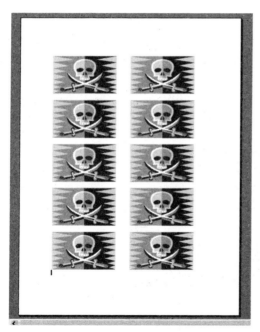

Fig.30 Copied and Pasted Clip Art

Copy Clip Art

Left-click on the clip art to
switch the grabs on.

Left-click on the **Copy** icon on the
Standard toolbar.

Use the **Tab** key, **space** bar and **return/enter** key to insert
spacing between the clip art.

Left-click on the **Paste** icon on the standard
toolbar.

The clip art will be inserted where the cursor is on the
document. Once you have copied the clip art you can left-
click on paste as many times as required.

Editing Clip Art

Clip Art can be edited, pieces of Clip Art not required can be deleted and sections of clipart can be repositioned, coloured, cut out and used.

Insert the clip art, put the mouse pointer over the clip art and right-click. A menu drops down. Left-click on **Edit Picture**. A square box appears around the picture.

Fig.31 Right-Click Menu

Fig.32 Square Box Grabs

Delete. Put the mouse pointer over the section of clip art to be deleted. Left-click; small grabs will appear around the section to be deleted. Press the **delete** key.

Reposition. Put the mouse over the section of clip art to be moved. Left-click and hold the mouse button down. Move by dragging to the new position.

Fig. 33 Repositioned Stars

Cut Out and Use. Put your mouse over the section of clip art to be cut out and used. Left-click and hold the mouse button down. Drag the required section away from the rest of the clip art. Right-click on the removed section and copy and paste it into the working document or delete the section not required.

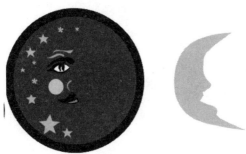

Fig.34 Cut out Moon

Colouring Clip Art

Insert the clip art. Put the mouse pointer over the clip art and right-click. A menu drops down. Left-click on **Edit Picture.** Put the mouse pointer over the section to colour and right-click. Left-click on **Edit Points.**

Fig.35 Right-Click Menu (Edit Points)

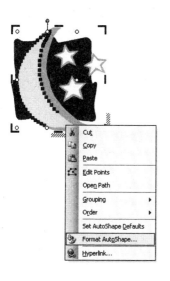

When the dots appear over the selected piece of clip art, right-click. In the drop-down menu left-click on **Format AutoShape**.

In the Format Auto shape window, left-click on the **Colours and Lines** Tab. Left-click on ∨ next to the **Color: box.** Left-click on the colour required and then left-click on **OK**.

Fig.36 Right-Click Menu (Format AutoShape)

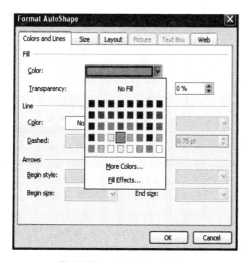

For a wider choice of colours Left-click on **More Colors**.
The colors window will open and display a colour chart.

Fig.37 Format AutoShape Menu

Left-click on a colour to choose it. The **new** colour will be displayed in the box, above the **current** colour. Left-click on **OK** to accept the colour or left-click on the colour chart again to choose a different colour.

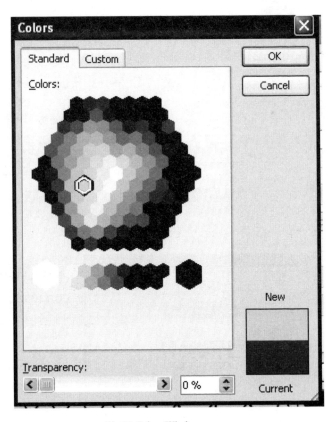

Fig.38 Colors Window

AutoShapes

There are two ways of inserting AutoShapes. Left-click on **AutoShapes** on the **drawing toolbar**.

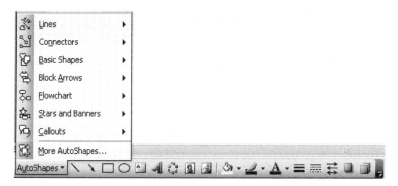

Fig.39 AutoShapes Menu (Drawing Toolbar)

Or left click on **Insert**, **Picture**, and **AutoShapes.**

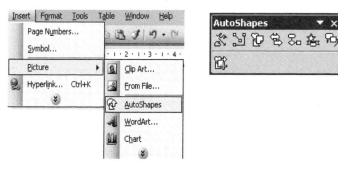

Fig.40 AutoShapes Menu (Insert Menu)

Clicking on the AutoShapes on the drawing toolbar will give you the icons and the names of the AutoShapes. Whereas using Insert, Picture, and AutoShapes will give you the AutoShapes toolbar with just the icons on it.

Insert AutoShape

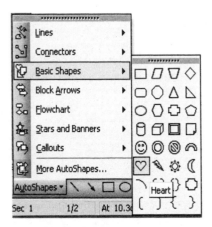

Fig.41 Basic Shapes Menu

Left-click on AutoShapes on the Drawing toolbar. Left-click on the type of AutoShape you require, e.g. Basic Shapes. Left-click on the AutoShape you have chosen e.g. Heart.

Fig.42 Drawing Box

When you have selected an AutoShape the mouse pointer will change from an arrow to a+. Place the + into the **Create your drawing here box** and left-click. The Create your drawing here box disappears and the AutoShape you have chosen appears with grabs around it.

The grabs are used to change the size, shape and position of the AutoShape. The Green dot at the top is used to rotate the AutoShape. To make the AutoShape:

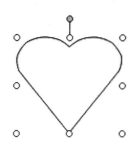

Bigger: Put your mouse pointer over one of the four corner grabs. Left-click and hold the mouse button down. Drag out to the size required.

Smaller: Put your mouse pointer over one of the four corner grabs. Left-click and hold the mouse button down. Drag in to the size required.

Wider: Put your mouse pointer over one of the two side and middle grabs. Left-click and hold the mouse button down. Drag in or out to the size required.

Longer: Put your mouse pointer over the top or bottom middle grabs. Left-click and hold the mouse button down. Drag up or down to the size required

Rotate: Put your mouse pointer over the Green grab. A curved arrow appears ↻.
Left-click and hold the mouse button down. Rotate to the position required.

Moving: AutoShapes can be moved by placing the mouse pointer over the AutoShape. When the mouse pointer changes to a four-pointed arrow, left-click and hold the mouse button down. Drag the AutoShape to the new position.

Colouring AutoShapes

AutoShapes can be coloured, filled and textured. Left-click on the AutoShape to switch the grabs on. Left-click on the ∨ next to the Bucket on the drawing toolbar. Left-click on a colour, left-click on **OK** to accept the colour or left-click on **More Fill Colours** or **Fill Effects.**

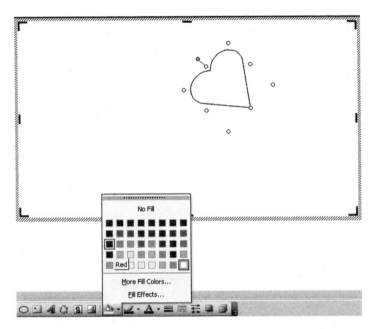

Fig.43 Fill Colour Menu

To remove the **Create your drawing here box,** left-click twice outside the box.

Heart AutoShapes resized, layered and coloured.

Fill Effects

Fill effects can be used on **Clip Art, Text Boxes**, and **Auto Shapes**. Insert the Clip Art, AutoShape or Text Box as usual. Put the mouse pointer over the image or Text box and right-click. A menu drops down. Left-click on **Format AutoShape.** In the Format Auto shape window, left-click on the **Colors and Lines** Tab. Left-click on ▼ next to the **Color:** box. Left-click on **Fill Effects**.

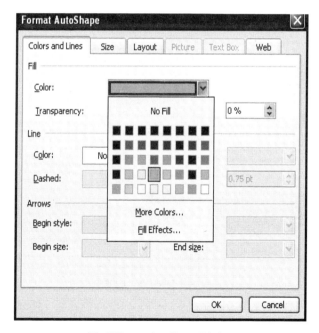

Fig.44 Format AutoShape Window

Gradient

Left-click on the **Gradient Tab**. Left-click on the circle to select one colour or two colours. Left-click on the ▼ in the colour boxes, this will automatically take you to the colour chart to choose new colours.

Left-click on the circle next to the **Shading style** required. The sample block will show you what the selected colours and shading style will look like. Left-click on **OK** to accept the selection. Left-click on **OK** in the Format Auto shape window.

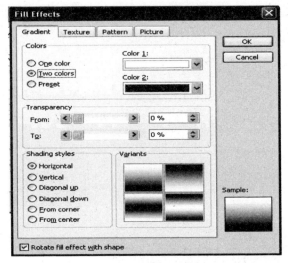

Fig.45 Fill Effects Window

An **AutoShape** heart combining, two colours, with **From corner** shading.

Texture

Left-click on the **Texture Tab**. Left-click on the texture to select it. Left-click on **OK** to apply the texture.

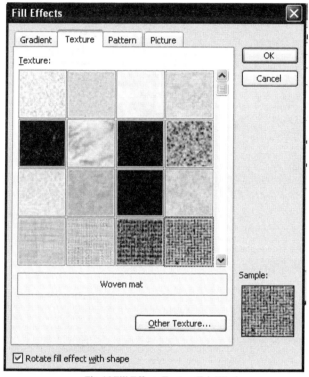

Fig.46 Fill Effects Texture Tab Window

Clip art shell on a woven mat background.

Pattern

Left-click on the **Pattern Tab**. Left-click on the pattern to select it. Left-click on the ∨ to change the Foreground and Background colours. Left-click on **OK** to apply the pattern.

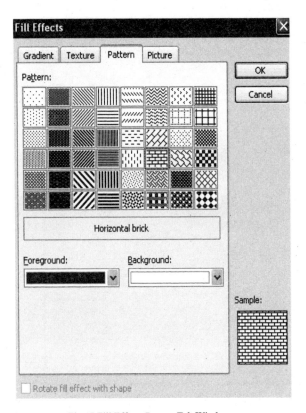

Fig.47 Fill Effects Pattern Tab Window

A patterned Text Box.

Washout

Left-click on the **Picture Tab**. Left-click on the ▼ next to **Color** under **Image Control**. Select **washout**. Alter the brightness and contrast if required. Left-click on **OK** to apply the washout.

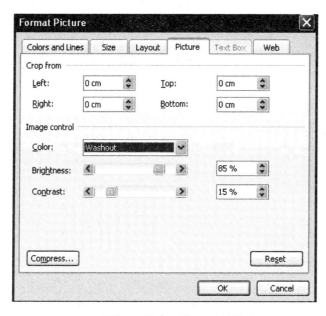

Fig.48 Format Picture, Picture Tab Window

Fig.49 Before Washout

Fig.50 After Washout

Exact Fit Auto Shapes

Insert the AutoShape. Left-click on the AutoShape to switch the grabs on.
Place your mouse on a grab and right-click.

Left-click on **Format AutoShape**.

In the **Format AutoShape** window, left-click on the **Size Tab.**

Height Box: Left-click on the ▲ up, and ▼ down arrows to enter the height you require.

Width box: Left-click on the ▲ up, and ▼ down arrows to enter the width you require. Left-click on **OK.**

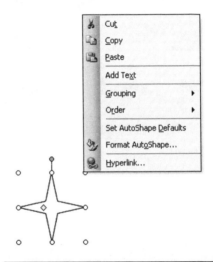

Fig.51 Format AutoShape, Size Tab Window

Your AutoShape will change to the required measurements. Insert pictures and colour as normal.

Add Text to an AutoShape

Insert the AutoShape. Left-click on the AutoShape to switch the grabs on.
Place your mouse on a grab and right-click.
Left-click on
Add Text.

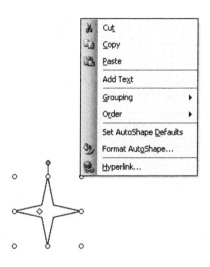

Fig.52 Right-Click Menu

The AutoShape acquires grabs and shading. The cursor is flashing ready for typing in the AutoShape. Reposition the cursor if required using the **Return/Enter** key.

Fig.53 AutoShape with Grabs and Shading

Type in and highlight the text. Change the Font Size, Font Style, and Font Colour if required. Use Bold, Underline and Italic as normal.

A Smiley AutoShape with Happy Chappy as Added Text and a coloured background.

CONGRATULATIONS
JULIE

ON PASSING YOUR
DRIVING TEST.

Banner AutoShape, with Added Text and changed Font styles.

Crop an image

Insert the image into the document. The image can be obtained from the Internet, clip art, scanner or digital camera.

Fig.54 Inserted Image

Left-click on the picture to **switch the grabs on.**
If the grabs are not switched on some of the icons on the picture toolbar will appear greyed out and not available to use.

On the picture toolbar left-click on the **crop icon**.

The mouse pointer turns from an arrow into the same overlapping square symbol which appears on the crop icon.

Place the square of the mouse pointer on top of the square grab on the picture. When they are lined up one on top of the other left-click and hold the mouse button down. Drag the grabs in to cut off the piece of image you do not require.

The excess background has been removed from the image.

Fig.55 Cropped Image

90° Rotate

Left-click on the image to switch the grabs on.

 Left-click on the **Rotate an image icon** on the picture toolbar.

Fig.56 Rotated Image

Each time you left-click on the rotate an image icon, the image will be rotated by 90°.

Transparent Colour

An interesting effect can
be obtained by adding
transparent colour.
Left-click on the image to
switch the grabs on.

Fig.57 Added Transparency

 Left-click on the **Set Transparent Color icon** on
the picture toolbar.

The mouse pointer turns from an arrow into the same pen-
like symbol which appears on the **Set transparent Color**
icon.
Place the pen of the mouse pointer on the image where you
want to set transparency and left-click the mouse button.
The chosen section of the image will have transparency
added. Repeat the process to further add transparency to the
image.

Contrast

Insert the image. Left-click on the image to switch the grabs on.

Left-click on the **More Contrast icon** on the picture toolbar; keep clicking until you have the required contrast.

Fig.58 Inserted Image

Fig.59 More Contrast

Left-click on the **Less Contrast icon** on the picture toolbar; keep clicking until you have the required contrast.

Fig.60 Less Contrast

Brightness

Insert the image. Left-click on the image to switch the grabs on.

Left-click on the **More Brightness icon** on the picture toolbar; keep clicking until you have the required brightness.

Left-click on the **Less Brightness icon** on the picture toolbar; keep clicking until you have the required brightness.

Fig.61 More Brightness

Fig.62 Less Brightness

Reset Picture

When you are manipulating images and you would like to return the image to its original form, i.e. as it was before you started changing it.

Left-click on the image to switch the grabs on.

Left-click on the **Reset Picture icon** on the picture toolbar and the picture will be changed back to how it appeared when you first inserted it.

Manipulating Text

Manipulating Text

When you first open a document or new page in Microsoft Word it is already preset (defaulted) for you. The writing will automatically be left aligned and in black. The font style will be Times New Roman and the font size will be 12pt.

There are a variety of ways of changing the text colour, size, position and style using the **Formatting Toolbar**.

Changing Text Style

Left-click on the ▼ in the Font style box to change the font style.

Left-click on the up arrow ▲ or the down arrow ▼ to scroll up and down the list of Font Styles.
Left-click on a **Font Style** to choose it.

Fig.63 Font Style Menu

Select a style before you start typing in your document and it will automatically type in the Font Style you have chosen. If you have already started typing, highlight the text first and then select a different Font Style.

Changing Text Size

Left-click on the ▼ in the Font size box to change the size of the text.

Left-click on the up arrow ▲ or the down arrow ▼ to scroll up and down the list of Font Sizes.

Left-click on a Font Size to choose it.

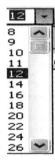

Fig.64 Font Size Menu

Bold Italic and Underline

The Bold Italic and Underline icons are like on/off switches. Left-click to switch on and left-click again to switch off. When they are switched on they have boxes around them.

Select bold, italic or underline before you start typing the text in your document and it will automatically type in the way you have chosen. If you have already started typing, highlight the text first and then select bold, italic or underline.

Alignment

Select the text alignment before you start typing in your document. The text will appear in the alignment position you have chosen. If you have already started typing, highlight the text first and then select the alignment required. You may want to use left alignment on one portion of text; and centre alignment on a different portion of text; if this is the case, highlight each section individually and left or centre align as appropriate.

The alignment icons are like on/off switches. Left-click to switch on and left-click again to switch off. When they are switched on they have boxes around them.

Left alignment switched on. (Box displayed) Text will appear on the left of document.

Centre alignment switched off. (Box not displayed) Text will appear in centre of document if switched on.

Right alignment switched off. (Box not displayed) Text will appear on right of document if switched on.

Justification alignment switched off. (Box not displayed) Text will appear squared on document if switched on.

Changing the Font Colour

Select the text colour before you start typing in your document. The text will appear in the colour you have chosen. If you have already started typing, highlight the text first and then select the colour required. You may want to use different colours on different portions of text and on individual words and letters. If that is the case, highlight each section or word individually and colour as appropriate.

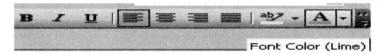

Font Color (Lime)

Fig.65 Formatting Toolbar Font Color Icon

The font colour is displayed beneath the letter A, in this case you would be typing in Lime Green.

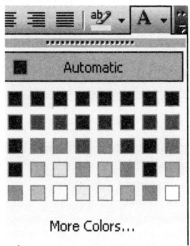

Left-click on the ▼ next to the Font Color icon and a drop-down menu will be displayed.

Left-click on the colour you want the text to be displayed in.

Left-click on **More Colors** to access the colour chart.

Fig.66 Font Colour Menu

Left-click on **Automatic** to change the Font colour back to black.

Copying and Pasting Text

Highlight the text to be copied. Left-click and hold the mouse button down, at the same time drag it across the text to be copied. It will turn black.

Left-click on the **Copy** icon on the **Standard Toolbar.**

Move the cursor to the place on the document you want to insert the copied text.

Left-click on the **Paste** icon on the **Standard Toolbar**.

The text will be inserted where the cursor is positioned on the document.

WordArt

 There are two ways of inserting WordArt. Left-click on the WordArt icon on the **drawing toolbar**.

Or left-click on **Insert**, **Picture**, and **WordArt.**

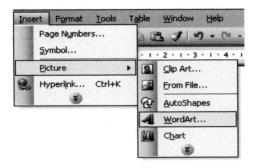

Fig.67 Insert Menu

In the WordArt Gallery, left-click on a WordArt style to select it. Left-click on **OK**

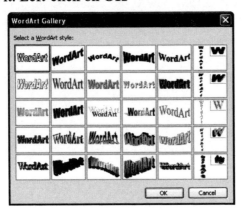

Fig.68 WordArt Window

Type in the text you want to be displayed in the WordArt format.

Fig.69 WordArt Text Box(Empty)

Left-click on the ▼ in the Font box to change the font style.
Left-click on the ▼ in the size box to change the size of the text.

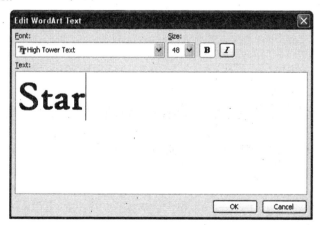

Fig.70 WordArt Text Box (With Text)

Left-click on **B** to embolden or *I* for italic writing.
Left-click on **OK** and the WordArt appears in the document.

Left-click on the WordArt to switch the grabs on. The grabs are used to change the size, shape and position of the WordArt.

Bigger: Put your mouse pointer over one of the four corner grabs. Left-click and hold the mouse button down. Drag out to the size required.

Smaller: Put your mouse pointer over one of the four corner grabs. Left-click and hold the mouse button down. Drag in to the size required.

Wider: Put your mouse pointer over one of the two side and middle grabs. Left-click and hold the mouse button down. Drag in or out to the size required.

Longer: Put your mouse pointer over the top or bottom middle grabs. Left-click and hold the mouse button down. Drag up or down to the size required

Moving: WordArt can be moved by using the space bar, and Return/Enter keys.

Changing: Left-click on the WordArt to switch the grabs on; at the same time as the grabs appear the WordArt toolbar pops up. The WordArt toolbar can be used to edit the text, choose a different gallery style, format, shape, text wrap, align and space out your text.

WordArt Toolbar

Left-click on the **WordArt icon** to change the gallery style and text.

Left-click on **Edit Text** to change or amend the text.

Left-click on the **WordArt Gallery icon** to change the style of the WordArt.

Left-click on the **Format WordArt icon** to access the Format WordArt window.

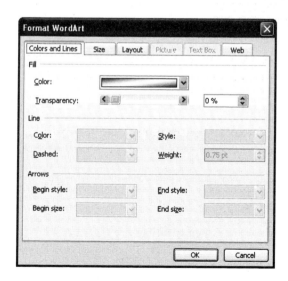

Fig.71 Format WordArt Window

In the Format WordArt window left-click on the **Colors and Lines** Tab.

Left-click on the ▼ in the Color box to access the Color Chart window and the Fill effects window. Refer to colouring AutoShapes for instructions on using the Color Chart and Fill Effects windows.

Line:
Left-click on the ▼ in the Color box to change the colour of the lines of the WordArt. Or choose **No Line** or **Patterned lines**.

Dashed: Left-click on the ▼ in the Dashed box to change the outline of the WordArt.

Size Tab: Left-click on the ▲ or ▼ to change the **Height** or **Width** of the WordArt.

Rotation:

Left-click on the up ▲ or down ▼ to rotate the WordArt.

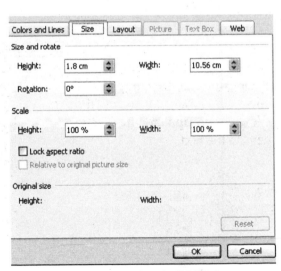

Fig.72 Format WordArt size Tab Window

WordArt Rotated 44°

Left-click on the **WordArt shape icon** to access the WordArt shape menu.

Left-click on a **shape** to select it. The WordArt changes to the shape selected.

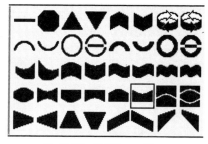

Fig.73 WordArt Shapes Menu

WordArt circle shape.

Left-click on the **Text Wrapping** icon (Dog). Left-click on how you want the WordArt to appear when it is next to the text.

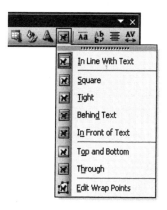

Fig.74 Text Wrapping Menu

Fig.75 WordArt placed Behind Text

Left-click on the **Same Letter Heights** icon to change the WordArt letters to the same height level.

Left-click on the **Vertical Text** icon to change the WordArt letters from Horizontal to Vertical.

Fig.77 Vertical

Fig.76 Horizontal

Left-click on the **WordArt alignment** icon. Left-click on an option to choose it.

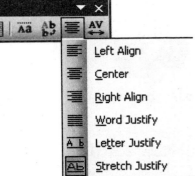

Fig.78 WordArt Alignment

Left-click on the **Character spacing** icon.

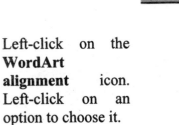

Fig.79 Normal Spacing

Fig.80 Very Loose Spacing

Fig.81 Character Spacing Menu

Shadows

Shadows can be put on Clip Art, WordArt and AutoShapes.
Left-click on the Clip Art, WordArt or AutoShape
to switch the grabs on. Left-click on the **Shadow style** icon on the **drawing toolbar**.

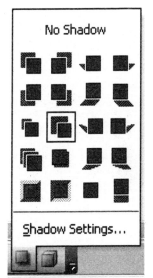

Fig.82 Shadow Menu

Left-click on a Shadow Style to select it.

The WordArt turns from:

To:

Fig.83 AutoShape smiley with shadow

3D

3D: Effects can be put on Clip Art, WordArt and
AutoShapes.
Left-click on the Clip Art, WordArt or AutoShape
to switch the grabs on. Left-click on the **3-D Settings** icon
on the **drawing toolbar**.

Fig.84 Shadow Menu

The WordArt turns from:

To:

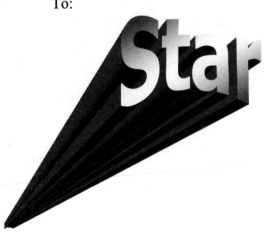

Rotating: Left-click on the word art to switch the grabs on. Put your mouse pointer over the Green grab. A curved arrow appears ↻.
Left-click and hold the mouse button down. Rotate to the position required.

Flipping: Rotate the text completely back to front.

Left-click to switch the grabs on. Put your mouse pointer on the grab in the middle on the bottom row. Left-click and hold the mouse button down. Pull straight up.

The text is upside down. Left-click on the Green Grab, and rotate the text until it is completely back to front.

The text is now ready to print to the paper.

Exact Fit Text Boxes

Measure your box or item across and down, keep a note of the measurements. The measurements will act as a guideline. You will need to have the drawing toolbar ready, see section on Toolbars if you do not have it already displayed.

Square Text Box

On the Draw Toolbar left-click on the Text Box icon

Your mouse pointer will turn to a +. Place the + where you want your box to appear, and left-click once.

The text box has squares or grabs and shading around it.
Place your mouse on the shaded area and right-click.

Left-click on Format Text Box.

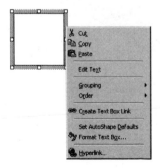

Fig.85 Right-Click Menu

In the **Format Text Box** window, left-click on the **Size Tab**

In the **Format Text Box** window you can increase the **Height and Width** of the text box by clicking on ▲, and decrease the **Height and Width** by clicking on ▼. Increase and decrease the **Height and Width** boxes to match your measurements. Place a tick in the **Lock Aspect Ratio Box** by left-clicking on the box. Left-click on **OK**.

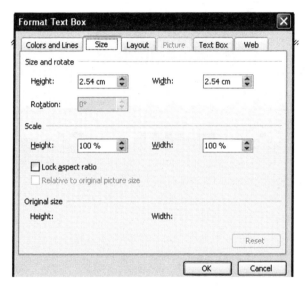

Fig.86 Format Text Box Size Tab Window

Your text box will change to the required measurements.

Print your empty text box and test it against your box or item for fit. Use the Format Text Box window to make any adjustments if required.

Left-click in the resized box, make sure your cursor is flashing. Insert a picture or text as normal. The picture will automatically resize itself to fit into the text box.

Fig.87 Text Box with inserted picture From File. With added WordArt.

Grids and Tables

Insert a Table

On the **Menu Bar** left-click on **Table, Insert** and **Table**.

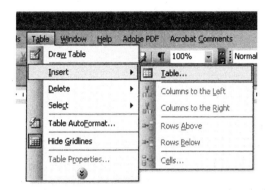

Fig.88 Table Menu

In the Insert Table window left-click on the ▲ up, and ▼ down arrows to enter the number of rows and columns you require.

Left-click on **OK**.

Fig.89 Insert Table Window

A three-column three-row table looks like this.

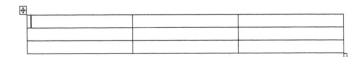

Manipulate the Table

Left-click on **Table** on the Menu Bar. Left-click on **Draw Table**.

The **Tables and Borders** Toolbar is displayed.

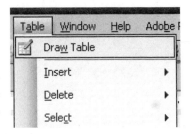

The mouse pointer turns to a pencil. Left-click and the mouse pointer returns to normal.

Highlight the Table. Left-lick on the cross in the square box at the corner of the table.

The Table turns Black.

Fig.90 Highlighted Table

Change the Width and Colour of the Gridlines

Highlight the Table. Left-click on the **Border Color** icon on the **Tables and Borders** Toolbar.

In the **Borders and Shading** window, left-click on the **Borders Tab.**

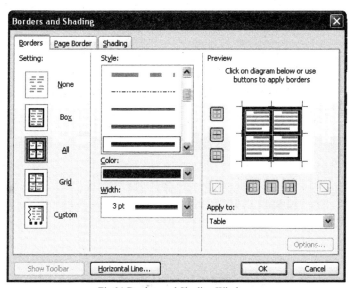

Fig.91 Borders and Shading Window

In the **Settings** section left-click on **All**.
In the **Style** section left-click on the ▲ up, and ▼ down arrows to view the style selection. Left-click on a style to select it.
In the **Color** section left-click on the ▼ down arrow to view the colour chart.
In the **Width** section left-click on the ▼ down arrow to view the line width selection.   The line width selection will vary depending on the style of line you have chosen.

The **Preview** section will change as you choose the options you want.

In the **Apply To** section: left-click on the ▼ down arrow and left click on **Table**.

Left-click on **OK** to apply the **Lines and Colours** to the Grid.

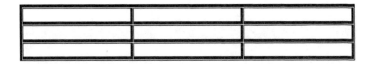

A three-column three-row table with line style and colour changed.

Change the Size of the Grid Cells

There are two ways to change the size of the grid cells.

Put the cursor into a cell and use the space bar and return/enter keys to enlarge the cell. Use the Tab key to move from cell to cell.

Change the Row Size

Put your mouse pointer onto a row. The mouse pointer changes to a two-pointed arrow. Hold the mouse pointer down. A line appears across the row to be altered. Move the line up or down to make the row bigger or smaller.

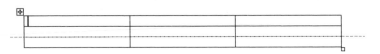

Fig.92 Table with sizing line switched on

Change the Column Size

Put your mouse pointer onto a column. The mouse pointer changes to a two-pointed arrow. Hold the mouse pointer down. A line appears across the column to be altered. Move the line up or down to make the column bigger or smaller.

Add Colour to the Grid Cells

Put the cursor into the cell to be coloured. Left-click on the ▼ down arrow next to the **Bucket** on the **Tables and Borders Toolbar.** Make sure you do not left-click on the Bucket on the Drawing

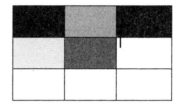

Toolbar. Left-click on a colour to select it.   Fig.93 Coloured Table

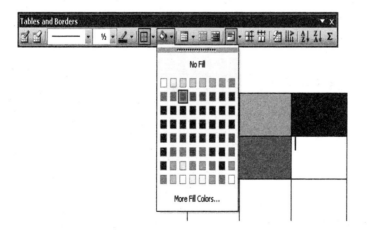

Fig.94 Table and Borders Toolbar with Fill Colour Menu displayed

Delete the Grid Lines

Highlight the Table. Left-click on the ▼ down
arrow next to the **All Borders** icon on the
Tables and Borders Toolbar.

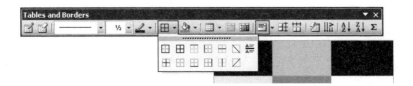

Fig..95 Table and Borders Toolbar with Border Menu displayed

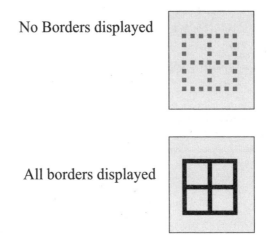

No Borders displayed

All borders displayed

Left-click on the menu grid to select which lines to delete
and which to display. When you choose **No Borders** the
grid appears greyed out. When you print the grid no lines
will be printed.

Craft Projects

Templates and Stencils

Templates

Templates are used for a wide variety of crafts. It is very useful to be able to make and keep your own stock of templates. You can use paper, card, fabric and acetate to print them out. Keep a copy of the original document as a template on file in your computer.

AutoShapes can be used for hearts, stars, squares, circles, and triangles.

ClipArt can be used for fish, flowers, moons, suns, leaves, shells, cherubs and fruit.

Wingdings and Webdings can be used for symbols including astrology, numbers and religious symbols. On the menu bar, left-click on **Insert, Symbol.** Then left-click on the symbol you require and left-click on **Insert** in the Symbol window.

Enlarge the symbol by highlighting the symbol and using the font size menu.

Stencils

For stencils use paper, card, and acetate. When using a repeat motif, e.g. for home decoration, print out on plain paper first and test for spacing and size.

Search clip art for Borders.

Black and white clip art and leaves clip art are good sources of motifs for stencils.

Borders and Shading is another good source for repeating motifs.

On the menu bar, left-click on **Format, Borders and Shading.**

Left-click on the **Page Border Tab**, left-click on the ▼ next to the **Art** section.

Use the scroll bars to move up and down.

Left-click on the Border you require and left-click on **OK** to insert the Border.

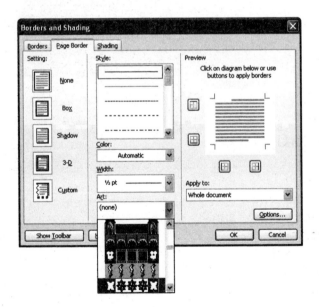

Fig.96   Borders and Shading page Border Tab Window

Decoupage Flowerpot

You will need

One Sheet of Plain Computer Paper
Scissors or Craft Knife
Quick drying Acrylic Varnish
Clay Flowerpot
White acrylic paint
Yellow acrylic paint
Kitchen Roll
Paintbrush
Water Based Glue

Decorate flowerpots by using acrylic paint in matching and contrasting colours and add an image to finish. Try experimenting with painted stripes, borders, small flowers, or giant sunflowers. Why not make a herb garden with a picture of the herb on the pot, or make a set of flowerpots to match your kitchen curtains. Acrylic paint is very versatile, dries quickly and can be painted over without the colour changing. After the flowerpot has been decorated and the glue has dried, apply a few thin coats of acrylic varnish to protect the image. Once the varnish has dried you can wipe the flowerpot with a damp cloth.

Painting the Flowerpot

1. Wash and dry the flowerpot.
2. Put the white acrylic paint on some screwed up kitchen roll and dab all over the flowerpot.
3. Leave to dry.
4. Put a strong yellow acrylic paint on a clean piece of screwed up kitchen roll and dab on top of the white paint.
5. Leave to dry.
6. Mix the white and yellow paint together and dab across the flowerpot.
7. Leave to dry.

Selecting and Applying the Image

1. Open a new Microsoft Word Document.
2. Open Clip art office online.
3. Enter a search for Flowers.
4. Select your images and download them onto your computer.
5. Search the clip art on your computer for Flowers.
6. Insert the chosen image into your document.
7. Adjust the size of the flowers by switching the grabs on and dragging the image to the required size.
8. Insert and adjust more images if required.
9. Test print on plain paper.
10. Make any adjustments needed.
11. Print on plain paper.
12. Save the work.
13. Leave to dry for 5 minutes.
14. Cut out the image and use water based glue to apply to the flowerpot.
15. Leave to dry thouroughly.
16. Apply quick drying acrylic varnish all over to protect the paint and images.

Embroidered Flower Card

You will need

Card with an Aperture
Computer Paper
Scissors
Needle
Silk Embroidery Thread
Tapestry Wool
Glue or Tape
Aida

Cards with apertures come in a great variety of sizes, shapes and colours. The cards are available in most craft shops, in packs with envelopes or individually. You can use this method to make key rings, book marks, to embroider pictures or design tapestries. It is excellent for black work pictures. Try experimenting with different count Aida.

1. Measure the card aperture.
2. Open a New Microsoft Word Document.
3. Set the Margins to 1cm.
4. Use the Exact Textbox method to create the proper size text box for the card aperture. Circle, oblong or square.

Print off the **empty** text box. Test it against the card aperture for size. Make any adjustments needed by changing the height and width measurements.

5. Copy and paste the textbox template if required.
6. Insert the Image, WordArt, Text or Picture.
7. Save the document.
8. Copy and paste the image, picture out of the text box.
9. Delete the text box.
10. Position the images on the document allowing a margin of Aida at the edge for fixing the Aida to the card.
11. Save the work.
12. Test and clean the printer.

Prepare the Aida

Cover the Aida material with a tea towel or kitchen paper and iron flat.

Place a sheet of A5, A4, or A3 computer paper on the Aida material and draw round it with a felt tip pen or ball point pen.

Cut the A5, A4 or A3 shape from the Aida material. Ensure that there are no bumps or jagged edges. Aim to make the edges as smooth as possible for easy passage through the printer.

Place the Aida in the printer between two sheets of computer paper and print.

Carefully cut out the printed images, allowing for edges.

Embroider and embellish the image. Glue or tape the finished embroidery to the card.

Shrink Badge, Necklace and Hairclip

You will need

Two Sheets of Computer Shrink Paper
One Sheet of Plain Computer Paper
Scissors or Craft Knife
Tin Foil
Heavy Book
Badge clip
Hair grip
Leather Thong or Jewellery Wire
Glue

Shrink paper can be used to make greetings card embellishments, buttons, badges, earrings, games counters and much more. Heating in an oven is involved in the shrink process and therefore children should be supervised at that stage. The process is the same for the badge, hairclip and necklace. The image will shrink a lot and the colours will darken. White will turn a grey yellow colour.

Shrink Badge

1. Open a new Microsoft Word Document.
2. Open Clip art office online.
3. Enter a search for Stars (the sheriff badge is under stars).
4. Select your images and download them onto your computer.
5. Search the clip art on your computer for Stars.
6. Insert the sheriff badge image into your document.
7. Enlarge the sheriff badge to approximately half a page.
8. Insert and adjust another image if required.
9. Test print on plain paper.
10. Make any adjustments needed.
11. Print on computer shrink paper.
12. Do not touch the image as it will smudge easily.
13. Leave to dry for approximately 15-30 minutes.

Heat the oven up 5 mins before putting the shrink paper in. Have a stand ready to put the hot baking tray on. A sheet of clean plain paper and a heavy book at least the size of the image to hand.

Shrinking the Paper

1. Cut out the sheriffs badge.
2. Heat the oven to 175°C or Gas Mark 3.
3. Line a baking tray with tin foil and place the sheriffs badge on top. Do not cover.
4. Put in the pre heated oven for 2 minutes.
5. Take the baking tray out of the oven and put on a stand.
6. Cover the shrink paper with the plain paper.
7. Put the heavy book on top of the plain paper and press down hard.
8. Remove the sheriffs badge from the baking tray and leave to cool.

The shrink paper will start to cool and become less pliable as soon as you remove it from the oven. As ovens vary, experiment with different temperatures until you have found the right shrinking temperature for your oven.

Shrink Necklace

Use the same process as the sheriff badge. After cutting out use a hole punch at the top centre to make a hole, do not make a hole too near the outside edge as it will easily snap after shrinking.

Shrink Hairclip

Use the same process as the sheriff badge. Glue onto a hair grip or hairclip.

Before Shrinking

After Shrinking

Fridge Magnets

You will need

One Sheet of Magnetic Computer Paper
One Sheet of Plain Computer Paper
Scissors or Craft Knife

Fridge magnets make ideal gifts for friends and family. They can be personalised with photographs, themed to individual hobbies and interests, and can also be used as an advertising tool. Fridge magnets are fun, quick and easy to do which makes them ideal for children to make.

Motorbike, Cat and Flower Magnets

The motorbike, cat and flower magnets use the same method.

1. Open a new Microsoft Word Document.
2. Download the image from the Internet or insert the image from clip art.
3. Resize the image and add any text required.
4. Print out a test sheet on plain computer paper.
5. Make any adjustments.
6. Save the document.
7. Test and clean the printer.
8. Remove any paper from the printer and insert the magnetic paper one sheet at a time.
9. Print the images.
10. Carefully cut round the images, leave a border if needed.

Smiley Magnet

1. Insert the Smiley AutoShape.
2. Resize the image and add any text required.
3. Format AutoShape.
4. In the Colors and Lines Tab
5. Choose Fill effects.
6. Two Colors.
7. Choose your colours.
8. In Shading styles choose diagonal down.

Photograph Magnet

1. Insert the AutoShape.
2. Resize the image.
3. Format AutoShape.
4. In the Colors and Lines Tab.
5. Choose Fill effects.
6. In the Fill Effects window left-click on the Picture Tab.
7. Left-click on Select Picture.
8. In the Select Picture Window, left-click on your picture to select it.
9. Left-click on Insert.

The picture will be inserted into the AutoShape.

Rainbow Magnet

1. Insert the rainbow clip art.
2. Resize the image.
3. Left-click, Edit Picture.
4. Left-click, Add Text.
5. Type in the text.
6. Change the font size, style, and centre the text.
7. Adjust the size of the text box if necessary.

Noughts and Crosses Magnetic Game

You will need

Magnetic Computer Paper
A Craft Knife and Cutting Mat
Ruler

Magnetic computer paper is slightly glossy, rubbery and thicker than paper. It goes through the printer as easily as normal paper. You will need to use the Tables and Borders toolbar, see section on Grids and Tables for full instructions. The following instructions are for a black and white board with red counters. Try experimenting with different coloured squares and counters.

Design the Board

1. Open a New Microsoft Word Document.
2. Set the Margins to 1cm.
3. Insert the Table. 3x3.
4. Change the gridlines from black to red.
5. Change the thickness of the gridlines.
6. Alter the dimensions of the grid/table to the size required for the board.
7. Change the grid cells/squares to black.
8. Change the grid lines to white.
9. Save the work.

Design the Counters

Use Capital letters for the O and X.

1. Type in an O and an X.
2. Highlight the O and X.
3. Left-click on the Bold icon.
4. Change the font to Arial.
5. Change the font colour to red.
6. Change the font size to fit your grid/square size.
7. Copy and Paste the counters 5 times.
8. Do a test print onto paper.
9. Make any changes required.
10. Save the work.
11. Test and clean the printer.
12. Print the document onto magnetic paper.
13. Leave to dry for 1 hour.
14. Cut round the counters and board using a ruler and craft knife.

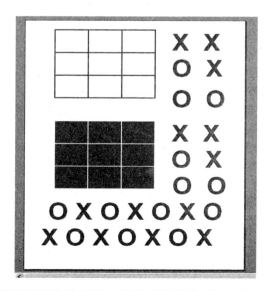

Fabric Horse Bag

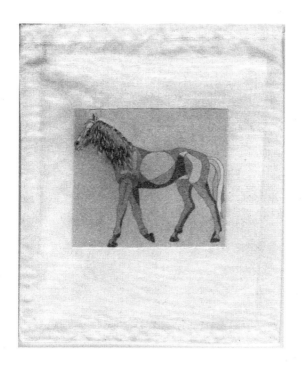

You will need

Fabric Bag
Computer Paper
Fabric Sheet
Scissors
Needle
Tapestry Wool
Fusible Bonding Web
Iron

Decorative Bags are very useful, easy and quick to decorate. You can make the bags in any size to suit your project needs. You can use plain or pre-printed fabric. Try laundry bags, shoe bags, PE bags, marble bags or toy bags. Add extra decoration by using tapestry wool, embroidery silks, beads, sequins, shells or netting.

1. Make or buy a fabric bag.
2. Open a New Microsoft Word Document.
3. Set the Margins to 1cm.
4. Download the horse clip art from Microsoft clip art online.
5. Add a background by using Format picture, and in the Colors and lines tab, choose a fill colour.
6. Adjust the image size to fit the bag.
7. Print a test page on paper.
8. Make any adjustments.
9. Save the document.
10. Test and clean the printer.

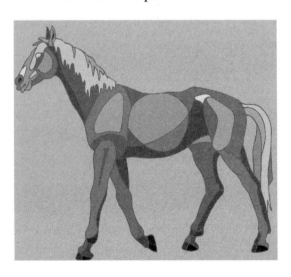

11. Print the image onto the fabric sheet.
12. Leave to dry for 15 minutes.
13. Remove the backing from the fabric sheet.
14. Iron the fusible bonding web onto the back of the image.
15. Cut out the image.
16. Remove the backing and iron onto the fabric bag.

The Mane

Using two strands of tapestry wool push the needle through the fabric from the front. Knot at the back. Continue until the mane is complete. Trim the mane to the length required.

Appliqué Underwater Scene

You will need

Computer Paper
Paper Glue
Fabric Sheet
Scissors
Needle
Tapestry Wool
Embroidery Silk
Beads
Fusible Bonding Web
Iron

Let your imagination run wild and have fun, use beads, quilting, glitter glue, embroidery silks, buttons, string, tapestry wool and bits of wood to create fabric pictures.
Make tablecloths, curtains, placemats, napkins and greetings cards.

The small underwater scene was made using a mixture of appliqué, embroidery and coloured beads. The fabric sheet used was a plain cotton sheet and fusible bonding web was inserted between the printed background and the fabric fish and shells. Iron-on cotton or adhesive-backed cotton might be a better choice depending on whether the finished item needs to be washed, as adhesive-backed cotton is not washable.

To make the underwater scene

1. Open a New Microsoft Word document.
2. Set the Margins to 0cm.

3. Insert the Blue Hills picture by left-clicking on Insert, Picture, From File, My Pictures, Sample Pictures, Blue Hills.
4. Resize the blue Hills picture to fit half the A4 page.
5. Download the shell, seaweed, swans and fish pictures from clip art online.
6. Change the colour of the seaweed to different shades of green.
7. Resize the shell, seaweed and fish clip art to fill the bottom half of the A4 paper.
8. Save the document.

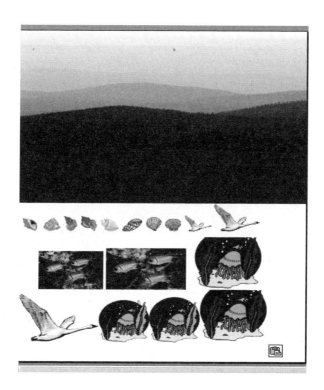

9. Test print on plain computer paper.
10. Cut out the paper background and the fish, shells, swans and seaweed shapes; arrange and glue onto the paper background.
11. Make any adjustments. Reprint on plain paper if necessary.
12. When you are happy with the colours and proportions of the picture you are ready to print onto the fabric.

13. Iron the fabric sheet if it is creased.
14. Put one fabric sheet in the paper feeder. If using more than one fabric sheet put them in the paper feeder one at a time.
15. Print the design.

With the backing paper still attached to the fabric

1. Cut out the background. You have two halves of A4.
2. Remove the backing paper from the shells, seaweed swans and fish section.
3. Keep the backing paper on the background section.
4. Do not cut out the shells, seaweed, swans and fish.
5. Iron the fusible bonding web to the back of the fabric.
6. Cut out the shells, seaweed, swans and fish.
7. Remove the fusible bonding web backing paper and iron the seaweed, shells, swans and fish in position. Use your paper copy as a guide.
8. Remove the backing paper from the background and iron.

Embellish the scene by using different lengths and colours of embroidery silk to make strands of seaweed.

Use tapestry wool for grains of sand. Add clear glass beads for bubbles and dark blue or dark green beads for interest.

Coloured Stained Glass Window Stickers

You will need

Computer Paper
Computer Window Cling
Scissors

Stained Glass window stickers are quick, easy and fun to make. These are ready coloured. Letters and numbers need to be reversed before printing.

1. Open a new Microsoft Word Document.
2. Open Clip art office online.
3. Enter a search for Stained Glass.
4. Select your images and download them onto your computer.
5. Search the clip art on your computer for stained glass.
6. Insert the chosen image onto your document.
7. Crop the image if neccessary.
8. Resize the image.
9. Place the image in position.
10. Insert more images if required.
11. Test print on plain paper.
12. Make any adjustments needed.
13. Save the work.
14. Print on computer window cling.
15. Leave to dry for one hour.
16. Cut out and use.

Black and White Stained Glass Window Stickers

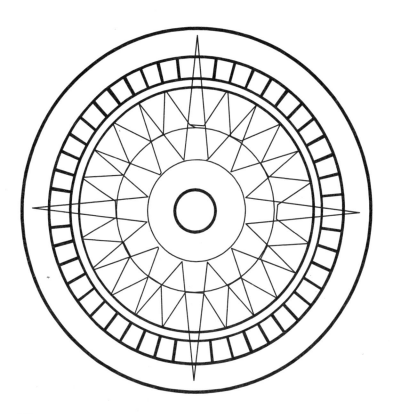

You will need

Computer Paper
Computer Window Cling
Scissors

Black and white Stained Glass window stickers can be printed off and coloured in using felt pens or permanent marker. Or you can colour them in via the computer and print them off pre-coloured. Reverse letters and numbers before printing.

1.   Open a new Microsoft Word Document.
2.   Open Clip art office online.
3.   Enter a search for Circles.
4.   Select your images and download them onto your computer.
5.   Search the clip art on your computer for circles.
6.   Insert the chosen image onto your document.
7.   Resize the circle.
8.   Put your mouse pointer on the circle and right-click.
9.   Left-click on Edit picture.
10. Left-click on the black triangles.
11. Right-click.
12. Left-click on Format AutoShape.
13. Left-click on the Colors and Lines Tab.
14. In the Line section. Under Color, use the drop-down menu and choose black.
15. In the Fill section use the drop-down menu and choose No Fill.
16. Repeat 14 and 15 if required.
17. Resize the image.
18. Place the image in position.
19. Insert more images if required.
20. Test print on plain paper.
21. Make any adjustments needed.
22. Save the work.
23. Print on computer window cling.
24. Leave to dry for one hour.
25. Colour.

Before editing.

After editing.

Car Window Sticker

You will need

Computer Paper
Computer Window Cling
Scissors

Autoshapes was used to create the basic design and shape of the car window sticker. Photographs, clip art, WordArt and AutoShapes can be combined to make more detailed window stickers. Remember to reverse the text before printing.

1. Open a new Microsoft Word Document.
2. Open AutoShapes.
3. In Basic Shapes choose the rounded rectangle.
4. Make a large rounded rectangle and place a smaller rounded rectangle in the position you want the text to be.
5. In AutoShapes Basic Shapes choose the smiley face and position above the smaller rounded rectangle.
6. Insert a Text Box in the smaller rounded rectangle.

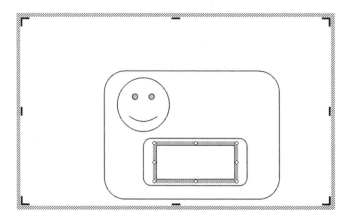

7. Left-click in the Text Box to activate the cursor.
8. Insert WordArt, Baby on Board.

9. Place the mouse on top of the WordArt and right-click.
10. Left-click on Format WordArt.

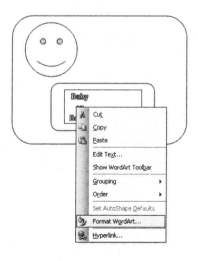

11. Left-click on the Colors and Lines tab.
12. In the Fill section left-click on the down arrow next to the Color section and choose Black.

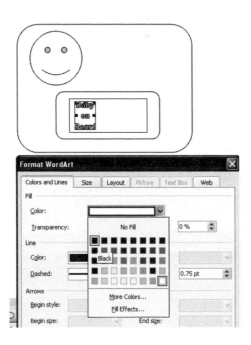

13. Left-click on the now-black Baby on Board text to switch the grabs on.
14. Fit the Baby on Board text to the rounded rectangle; alter the size of the text box if necessary.
15. Flip and Rotate the WordArt to reverse the text.

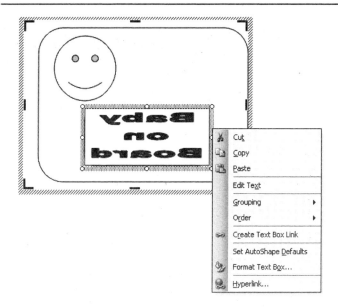

16. Left-click on the Text box to switch the grabs on.
17. Right-click to access the menu.
18. Left-click on Format Text Box.
19. Left-click on the Colors and Lines tab.
20. In the Line section left-click on the down arrow next to the Color section and choose No Line.

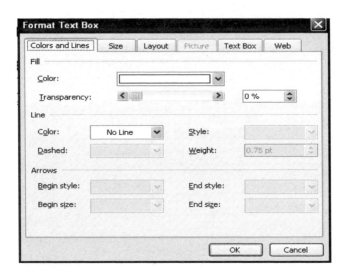

21. Left-click in the large rounded rectangle.
22. Left-click on the fill color on the drawing toolbar.
23. Choose yellow.
24. Or: Right-click on the rounded rectangle and left-click on Format AutoShape. Left-click on the Colors and Lines tab and in the Fill section left-click on the down arrow next to the Color section and choose Yellow.
25. Repeat in the smaller rounded rectangle.
26. Test print on plain paper.
27. Make any adjustments needed.
28. Save the work.
29. Print on computer window cling.
30. Leave to dry.

Decorating Candles

You will need

One Sheet of Water Slip Decal Computer Paper
One Sheet of Plain Computer Paper
Scissors or Craft Knife
Acrylic Varnish
Candle
Bowl of Water
Soft Cloth

Clear Computer Water Slip Decal Paper has been used to decorate a small box of pastel coloured candles with Fruit images. Images produced using the clear water slip decal paper do not contain the colour white and have a clear background which does not show when applied to a product. Images produced using the white water slip decal paper will print the colour white and have a white background which must be cut off or it will show if not part of the design.

Sizing the Image

1. Open a new Microsoft Word Document.
2. Open Clip art office online.
3. Enter a search for Fruit.
4. Select your images and download them onto your computer.
5. Search the clip art on your computer for Fruit.
6. Insert the chosen image into your document.
7. Measure the candle and decide how big you want the image.
8. Right-click on the image.
9. Left-click on Format Picture.
10. Left-click on the Size Tab.
11. In the Size and Rotate section use the arrows to change the Height and Width of the image.
12. If the image is not quite right untick the Lock Aspect Ratio Box under the Scale section.
13. Add a background, border or WordArt if required.
14. Insert and adjust more images if required.
15. Test print on plain paper.
16. Make any adjustments needed,
17. Print on computer water slip decal paper.
18. Leave to dry.

1.

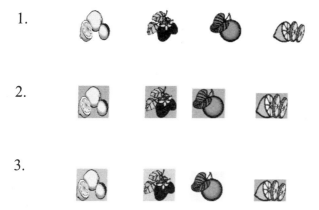

2.

3.

Fruit Water Slip Decals ready to print.

1. No background.
2. Green backgrounds.
3. Various coloured backgrounds.

Water slip decal paper is very sticky when wet and will flop over and stick to itself. Once applied to a surface it is quite manoeuverable and with a light touch can easily be repositioned.

Transferring the Decal to the Candle

1. Lightly spray the computer decal paper with acrylic varnish.
2. Leave to dry for 5 minutes, spray and dry twice more, leave to dry for 60 minutes.
3. Cut out the image.
4. Put one decal at a time into a bowl of water.
5. Leave in the water for 30-45 seconds.
6. Remove and shake off the excess water.
7. Do not remove the backing paper.
8. Peel a small part of the backing paper down.
9. Place the peeled part of the decal in position on the candle.
10. Carefully pull the rest of the backing paper away at the same time as positioning the decal on the candle.
11. Carefully adjust the decal if needed.
12. Using a soft dry cloth remove any air bubbles and water.
13. Leave to dry for 12-24 hours depending on the temperature.
14. Apply acrylic varnish to protect the image.

Teapot

You will need

One Sheet of Water Slip Decal Computer Paper
One Sheet of Plain Computer Paper
Scissors or Craft Knife
Acrylic Spray Varnish
Teapot or Ceramic
Bowl of Water
Soft Cloth

Decorate teapots and matching cups and saucers to make a bespoke dinner service. Clear water slip decal paper has been used to decorate the teapot. After the decal has been applied and thoroughly dried, apply a few thin coats of acrylic varnish to protect the decal, you can wipe the ceramic with a damp cloth but it is not dishwasher proof.

Sizing the Image

1. Open a new Microsoft Word Document.
2. Open Clip art office online.
3. Enter a search for Tea or Coffee.
4. Select your images and download them onto your computer.
5. Search the clip art on your computer for Tea or Coffee.
6. Insert the chosen image into your document.
7. Measure the teapot, cup or plate and decide how large you want the image.
8. Right-click on the image.
9. Left-click on Format Picture.
10. Left-click on the Size Tab.
11. In the Size and Rotate section use the arrows to change the Height and Width of the image.
12. If the image is not quite right untick the Lock Aspect Ratio Box under the Scale section.
13. Add a background, border or WordArt if wanted.
14. Insert and adjust more images if required.
15. Test print on plain paper.
16. Make any adjustments needed,
17. Print on computer water slip decal paper.
18. Leave to dry for 12-24 hours depending on the temperature.

Some Clip Art images can be used for both tea and coffee. Use the images on cups and saucers or try a completely different approach such as fruit, animals, or spirals.

Transferring the Image to the Ceramic

1. Lightly spray the computer decal paper with acrylic varnish.
2. Leave to dry for 5 minutes, spray and dry twice more, leave to dry for 60 minutes.
3. Cut out the image.
4. Put one decal at a time into a bowl of water.
5. Leave in the water for 30-45 seconds.
6. Remove and shake off the excess water.
7. Do not remove the backing paper.
8. Peel a small part of the backing paper down.
9. Place the peeled part of the decal in position on the teapot.
10. Carefully pull the rest of the backing paper away at the same time as positioning the decal on the teapot.
11. Carefully adjust the decal if needed.
12. Using a soft dry cloth remove any air bubbles and water.
13. Leave to dry for 12-24 hours depending on the temperature.
14. Apply two coats of acrylic varnish to protect the image on the ceramic.

Spiral Glasses

You will need

One Sheet of Water Slip Decal Computer Paper
One Sheet of Plain Computer Paper
Scissors or Craft Knife
Acrylic Varnish
Glasses
Bowl of Water
Soft Cloth

Use Clear Computer Water Slip Decal Paper to decorate drinking glasses. Choose a spiral image and use the Edit picture facility to change the colour of the spirals.

Sizing the Image

1. Open a new Microsoft Word Document.
2. Open Clip art office online.
3. Enter a search for Spirals.
4. Select your images and download them onto your computer.
5. Search the clip art on your computer for Spirals.
6. Insert the chosen image into your document.
7. Measure the glasses and decide how large you want the images.
8. Right-click on the image.
9. Left-click on Edit Picture.
10. Put the mouse pointer on top of the spiral and right-click.
11. Left-click on Format Auto Shape.
12. Left-click the Colors and Lines Tab.
13. In the Fill section use the down arrow to change the colour of the spiral.
14. Insert and change more spirals.
15. Test print on plain paper.
16. Make any adjustments needed.
17. Save the work.
18. Print on computer water slip decal paper.
19. Leave to dry for 12-24 hours depending on the temperature.
20. Apply two coats of acrylic varnish to protect the images on the glasses.

Water slip decal paper is very sticky when wet and will flop over and stick to itself. Once applied to a surface it is quite manoeuverable and with a light touch can easily be repositioned.

Transferring the Spiral to the Glass

1. Lightly spray the computer decal paper with acrylic varnish.
2. Leave to dry for 5 minutes, spray and dry twice more, leave to dry for 60 minutes.
3. Cut out the spirals.
4. Put one decal at a time into a bowl of water.
5. Leave in the water for 30-45 seconds.
6. Remove and shake off the excess water.
7. Do not remove the backing paper.
8. Peel a small part of the backing paper down.
9. Place the peeled part of the decal in position on the glass.
10. Carefully pull the rest of the backing paper away at the same time as positioning the decal on the glass.
11. Carefully adjust the decal if needed.
12. Using a soft dry cloth remove any air bubbles and water.
13. Repeat using random spiral colours all over the glass.
14. Leave to dry for 12-24 hours depending on the temperature.
15. Apply acrylic varnish to protect the image.

Princess T-Shirt

You will need

One Sheet of Plain Computer Paper
One Sheet of computer Heat Transfer Paper (Light)
Scissors
White or Light Coloured T-Shirt
Iron
Large Sheet of Paper or a large Cloth or Kitchen Roll
Table
Baking Parchment

T-Shirts are fun to design especially for children. Use photographs, clip art, WordArt or a design package.You can make matching T-shirt designs for your club or team, or personalise childrens T-shirts for a gift. Heat transfer paper can be used to decorate most fabrics including curtains, quilts, table cloths, napkins, and bibs. The longer you iron the paper on to the fabric the better it will withstand washing.

Prepare the T-shirt by washing and ironing it to remove any finish put on by the manufacturer.

Designing the Image

1. Open a new Microsoft Word Document.
2. Open Clip art office online.
3. Enter a search for Princess.
4. Select your images and download them onto your computer.
5. Search the clip art on your computer for Princess.
6. Insert the chosen image into your document.
7. Enlarge the image.
8. Insert the WordArt.
9. Format the WordArt to change the colour and shape.
10. Place the WordArt in position.
11. Add a background or Border if required.
12. Test print on plain paper.
13. Make any adjustments needed.
14. Save the work.
15. Print on Computer Heat Transfer Paper.
16. Leave to dry for 5 minutes.

Transferring the Image to The Fabric

Using a table allows you to press harder on the T-shirt with the iron and will make a better transfer. Protect the table from the heat of the iron by using a large sheet of paper, a towel, or kitchen roll. Put the iron on the hottest setting and switch the steam off. When ironing press down hard and iron for at least 2 minutes to set the image.

1. Use the test print to determine the position of the image on the T-shirt.
2. Cut out the image.
3. Protect the table.
4. Put the T-shirt on the table face up.
5. Remove the backing paper from the image.
6. Place the cut-out image printed side up, facing you in position on the T-shirt.
7. Put the baking parchment over the image.
8. Heat the iron on the hottest setting.
9. Press down hard and iron the image protected by the baking parchment for at least 2 minutes.
10. Leave to cool.
11. Remove the baking parchment.

Door Number Plaque

You will need

Two Sheets of Plain Computer Paper
One Sheet of Computer Dry Rub Off Decal paper
One Sheet of Computer Shrink Paper
Scissors or Craft Knife
Wooden Plaque
Acrylic Spray Varnish
White acrylic paint
Paintbrush
PVA Glue

Dry Rub Off decals are very versatile and can be used on nearly any surface. When using them on painted surfaces pay extra attention to positioning the decal, as the very sticky backing on the decal will remove the paint if peeled off to repostion the decal.

Painting the Wooden Plaque

1. Remove any varnish and rub with sandpaper if necessary.
2. Paint with one coat of undiluted white acrylic paint.
3. Leave to dry.
4. Spray with acrylic varnish.
5. Leave to dry for at least one hour.

Selecting the Image

1. Open a new Microsoft Word Document.
2. Open Clip art office online.
3. Enter a search for Borders.
4. Select your images and download them onto your computer.
5. Search the clip art on your computer for Borders.
6. Insert the chosen image into your document.
7. Measure the Plaque and decide how large you want the image.
8. Right-click on the image.
9. Left-click on Format Picture.
10. Left-click on the Size Tab.
11. In the Size and Rotate section use the arrows to change the Height and Width of the image.
12. If the image is not quite right untick the Lock Aspect Ratio Box under the Scale section.
13. Insert and adjust more images if required.
14. Test print on plain paper.
15. Make any adjustments needed.
16. Save the work.

Insert the Number

1. Insert the WordArt.
2. Use the blank block lettering WordArt and type in the number 7 instead of text.
3. Right-click on the number seven to turn the grabs on.
4. Left-click on Format WordArt.
5. Left-click on the Layout Tab.
6. Left-click on In Front of Text.
7. Left-click on OK.

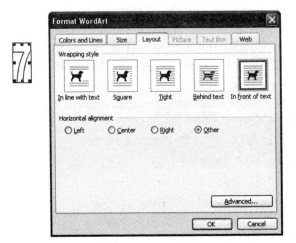

8. Place the number seven WordArt on top of the Border.

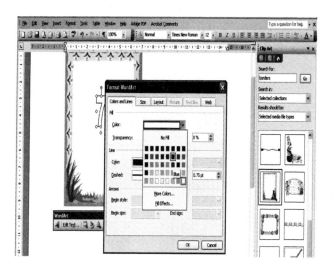

9. Right-click on the number seven to turn the grabs on.
10. Left-click on Format WordArt.
11. Left-click on the Colors and Lines Tab.
12. Left-click on the down arrow next to the color box.
13. Left-click on dark blue.
14. Left-click on OK.
15. Resize the number Seven to fit in the border square.
16. Reverse the number seven.
17. Test print on plain paper.
18. Make any adjustments needed.
19. Save the document.
20. Print on Computer Dry Rub Off Decal Paper.
21. Leave to dry for 1 hour.

The Butterflies

Refer to the shrink necklace, badge and hairclip instructions. Each butterfly is approximately half an A4 size on the shrink paper before being shrunk.

Transferring the Image to the Plaque

1. Put the number plaque image printed side up facng you.
2. Gradually peel the backing paper from the adhesive sheet which comes with the dry rub off decal paper and press onto the printed image.
3. Work slowly, use a roller and remove any air bubbles with a soft cloth as you go.
4. When the adhesive paper has been attached to the printed image and the air bubbles removed leave for at least 1 hour.
5. Cut out the image.
6. Peel the shiny backing paper from the cut-out image.
7. Position the decal carefully as you place it sticky side down onto the plaque.
8. Rub the decal hard with a soft cloth to transfer the image onto the plaque.
9. Peel off the plastic backing.
10. The decal will gradually harden.

Finishing Touches

Spray with acrylic varnish and when dry, use PVA glue to attach the butterflies.

Gift Boxes

You will need

Cardboard Boxes
Acrylic Paint
Paintbrush
Computer Paper
Scissors or a Craft Knife
Cutting mat if using a Craft Knife
Acrylic Varnish

These versatile cardboard boxes are available from most craft shops and come in a variety of shapes and sizes. They make great gifts themselves but are even better when holding small treats or surprises. Personalise them with names and dates, or use for children's parties.

Acrylic paint dries quickly so mix enough paint for two or three coats of each box and use a damp cloth or wet kitchen paper to cover the unused paint in between coats. Give each box at least two coats of acrylic paint inside and out. Leave the box to dry thoroughly between coats. Try painting a selection of boxes, once painted you can keep them and add the decoration at a later date.

Measure your box across and down; keep a note of the measurements. This will act as a guideline. You will need to use the drawing toolbar, see section on Toolbars if you do not have the drawing toolbar already displayed.

Painting the Boxes

1. Measure the boxes.
2. Give each box two coats of Acrylic paint.
3. Leave to dry between coats.

Selecting the Image

1. Open a New Microsoft Word Document.
2. Set the Margins to 1cm.
3. Use the Exact AutoShape or the Exact Textbox method to create the proper size box or AutoShape to fit the measurements of the boxes.

Print the empty text box or AutoShape. Test it against your box for size. Make any adjustments needed by changing the height and width measurements. When you are happy with the measurements save and name the document **square box template.** The template can be reused over and over again. After you have inserted the images save the template with a different name. You will have the original template and a copy with the images inserted.

4. Copy and paste the template if required.
5. Insert the Image, WordArt, Text or Picture.

6. Save the document.
7. Test and clean the printer.
8. Print the document.
9. Carefully cut around the images.
10. Use water based paper glue to stick the images to the boxes.
11. Smooth out any air bubbles using a soft cloth or roller.
12. When the glue is completely dry give each box two coats of quick drying acrylic varnish.

The amount of boxes you can fit onto a page will depend on the box size and shape.

Index